Poems From The Throne Room

Poems From The Throne Room
By Latrice Terrell

Copyright@ 2019 by Latrice Terrell.

Published By Latrice Terrell.

Under Sophisticated Press LLC.

PRINTED IN THE UNITED STATES OF AMERICA.

Book Design By: Sophisticated Press LLC.

ISBN 978-0-12345678-9-0

Acknowledgment

I thank God for gifting me with the love of poetry and writing. One thing I have always done was write. Ever since I was a young teen I wrote about everything and kept a journal with me. I always took notes in church and eventually my closet had a stack of notebooks filled with the voice of God speaking through me, just not released to the world. I love the way God speaks and I am happy that he chose to speak through me. I thank God for this gift because this is a beautiful way to share Jesus Christ with the world.

Table of Contents

Introduction 1
The Struggle 2
Inconsistency 4
The Perfect Christian 6
Temporary Fix 8
Love Drunk 10
Unequally Yoked 12
Distracted by my Desires 13
Reset 18
Wait on the Lord 20
Dispense 22
Breakthrough 24
Oil Spill 26
Saturated 28
Awakened 30
Amber Alert 32
The Library of Heaven 33
Glimpse 36
Perfect Love 38
Undefeated 41
Exposing the Enemy 43
Identity Thief 47
Deceived 50
About The Author 53

Introduction

This is a collection of poetry. The poems, prayers, and declarations in this book are to help you get back to your God given Identity. God created our identity when he created us. For some of us, like myself, our identity can get lost along the journey of life. We end up not knowing who we really are or where to go. We are lost. Searching for our identity in all the wrong places, other people, and things. Some of us know our identity but run from it and think we can live outside of it. This book will challenge you to ask yourself critical questions about who you really are. Who are you before traumatic experiences? Who are you before someone spoke something over you? Who are you before the world deceived you? After each poem I encourage you to write down key points. If you find something that you struggle with go to God in prayer and ask him for help. Open up your Bible or get one and study the word of God. This is simply making a choice to live in your God given identity daily, consistently, and wholeheartedly.

The Struggle

This journey of getting back to my identity was a struggle. I'm not going to sugar coat it. I am going to be honest and transparent because you maybe in a similar situation. This is my story and I am sharing it with you to help get you back to Jesus Christ. I grew up in church. My family always went and we believed in God. So I knew of God but I struggled with my relationship with Him off and on. I was always struggling with what I wanted and seeking to live for God. It felt like a constant battle of doing what I wanted and what God would be pleased with. I "backslid" all the time. I would go to God and ask Him for help. I would apologize and end up back asking for help. I was stuck in a cycle and for years kept failing the same test not realizing I was being tested. My perception of God was based off of my family, pastors, other ministers, Periscopes, and Facebook lives. I was so lost. I was struggling with sexual sin. I struggled with pornography. I struggled with relationships with guys. I struggled in my relationship with my family. I struggled with school. I struggled. I felt overwhelmed. Sometimes I felt like I would always struggle with the same things…

Inconsistency

Why does inconsistency happen consistently?

I am sick of the sometimes,

Tired of the maybe's,

and completely done with the every now and then.

I want to be in a continuous flow of growth.

If you try to come into my life just to inconsistently pop up from time to time,

You might as well stay out.

Inconsistency I don't want you.

I am leaving you and the guy you showed up with at the door.

Inconsistency, you are left on read,

Blocked,

and deleted.

You will never take my time, my morals, or my life.

I use to entertain you,

I was lost in you.

Now, I am found in Jesus Christ.

Now, I consistently say no to inconsistency.

The Perfect Christian

The perfect Christian does not exist…

Why?

No one is perfect,

if you were you would not need God.

You probably would not come to God because we go to God knowing we aren't perfect, but we are made perfect in his image.

God is looking for those who are not perfect

But..

are seeking his perfect will.

In the Bible it says His ways are perfect. His Word is tried and He is a shield to all who trust in him (2Samuel 22:31).

God knows you are not perfect.

God sees you perfectly imperfect and yet, He gives you access to his perfect love.

His perfect son Jesus died for you and He has a perfect plan for you.

Do not measure your life or what God can do for you by worldly standards.

You are not made perfect by the way you dress or how much money you have.

You were created by a perfect God who is perfect in all his ways.

Do not wait to realize your identity in Jesus Christ.

Coming to God is not something you prepare for,

It is a decision.

It's taking action and choosing how you will live daily.

You do not look like other Christians because you were never designed to,

God created you different.

God does not require church clothes or religious laws to belittle those who are often labeled different.

God wants you.

He wants a relationship with you,

Choose.

Temporary Fix

God is not interested in being a temporary fix,

God is looking for those who will submit their whole life to Him..

Not a few days,

Not until we get what we are praying for,

But God is looking for a relationship.

Intimacy.

God is a jealous God,

It Is

All Or

Nothing,

Choose.

No more half way or being on the fence,

God wants you to trust Him and go to Him for everything.

God wants you to seek after Him,

Do not just use God to get what you want.

We don't like when people treat us that way in a relationship,

Yet

We treat God like this all the time.

spend time in his presence,

Talk to Abba,

and listen.

Worship Him,

and read the Word.

Do not give up after a few days or a few months.

Apply consistency and

go to God daily.

Choose.

Love Drunk

Maybe I was too drunk off of emotions to see the devil sent a beautiful counterfeit of what I thought was an answered prayer.

I mean I wasn't drunk..I was just tipsy…

They knew just what to say..

-SIP.

They made me laugh..

-SIP.

They went to church..

-SIP.

They talked about God.. sometimes..

-SIP.

We talked on the phone for hours..

-SIP.

I got dressed up for church so they could notice me. instead of being focused on God…

-SIP.

....

We had sex.

-DRUNK!

We kept having sex…

-soul tie

Heart fragmented..

Being love drunk took 3 years to heal from. I didn't know what a soul tie was, so I thought the constant thoughts of this guy were normal.

My soul was still tied to his soul after years of not seeing Him. I had dreams of Him. I kept checking his social media. I couldn't get Him out of my mind.

I prayed..

and prayed, but I couldn't stop thinking about him. He was the first guy I loved. Once I understood that I had a soul tie I had to fast and pray. I had to speak Psalms 23 over myself Daily. I had to heal.

Unequally Yoked

When it comes to a relationship it will never be the right time for the wrong person.

The more you try to hold on,

the greater the loss and the deeper the hurt.

Learn how to be patient while you wait on God to bless you with the right one.

Do not go looking for love in the wrong places.

Look to God,

Focus on meeting your own requirements you ask for,

Work on you, and be happy.

True happiness comes from within and does not need any validation from others.

Work on your relationship with God first,

God knows you want to get married.

Learn to trust God,

It is worth the wait!

Distracted by my Desires

I want to get married one day,

I really do.

It is one of my goals.

I'm denying my flesh.

I'm studying the Word of God.

I'm putting in time and effort.

I'm sacrificing.

The question is,

am I preparing myself for a man, but losing sight of God?

Why do I want to be married?

Do I just want to get married for the benefits?

Am I searching for love?

Am I using God just to get what I want?

Am I only studying the Bible to get what I pray for, while forgetting who I am praying to?

What are my motives?

Who am I worshiping?

Who is getting the glory?

Why do I want to get married?

Why am I seeking a relationship with man if I don't have one with God?

Why is my heart's desire becoming a distraction?

Is my future husband an idol now?

Why am I meditating and thinking about this more than the word of God?

I spend so much time on social media liking status and memes about love, but I only pray for a few minutes.

I'm sorry God,

forgive me.

I repent.

I realize that my hearts desires are now distractions.

Because my focus was on you God,

But..

My thoughts shifted my view and I let fear and doubt turn me in a new direction.

So I'm still walking, but now I'm sideways, side tracked, and stuck in the wrong lane of traffic.

Why,

Because I got off on the wrong exit into a place where I don't belong.

I'm lost.

I was focused on you God, but my hearts desires distracted me and I began to listen when they spoke to me.

I started following them as my GPS instead of you.

Now I look like I'm following you, but I got off on the wrong exit.

I ended up in a detour of the wrong relationship.

I had sex and that led me into a foggy place.

Now questioning my identity because I lost a piece of myself to him.

I'm swerving into the unknown on backroads.

I still think of you from time to time God.

I might open my Bible.

I might go to church,

But I'm still,

Lost.

When you are driving down the road you do not "look" lost to others.

So others follow you because they are lost too and trying to find a way back to God.

Our discernment was the warning signs letting us know the speeding limit, a stop sign, a do not enter sign, and a turn-around because a cliff is ahead sign.

Our desires became distractions and we lost sight of God.

We turned off our GPS because we thought we knew where we were going.

We got lost.

Even in a lost place you can turn on your GPS and get back on track.

No matter how far you get from God,

He can reel you back in.

All it takes is a decision.

Focus on God and even if you feel like You can't hear Him or see Him, get closer until He is in your view.

Sometimes we don't realize that when we focus on God, He will give us the desires of our heart.

Choose.

Reset

Let the sweet presence of God captivate you

Let Jesus tickle your beautiful mind

Listen to the gentle whispers of God

Let words soft as lavender caress you

In the presences of God feel his love

As it pours into you like faint rain drops

Allow Jesus to blanket you in his arms

Let the wisdom of God set your sail

Let his voice lead you into still waters and up peaceful streams

As you surrender to God take his hand

Let God lead you to heaven

Elevate your mind and focus on God

Focus your eyes on healing, transformation, and knowledge

Walk on water and never look down

Take your sword, put on your armor, and hold your shield

Let the instructions of the Lord fill your ears

Let God reset your mind

Lift your hands to the heart beat of heaven

Worship God with a beautiful fragrance of love

Let the sweet honey of God pour and overflow your spirit

Speak the language of love seasoned with light

Reset your seed

Bloom!

Wait on the Lord

I wait on the Lord with a smile on my face.

I have joy in my heart,

for I know what God has for me is the best of the best.

The ultimate surprise,

so I wait on the Lord with closed eyes.
Hands lifted in worship and praise,

I say my prayer and stand firm on the word of God.

My Spirit leaps with confidence and faith.

I anticipate the will of God.

With all negativity behind me,

I focus on you Jesus.

I look to you.

I wait,

just a little longer..

I stay anchored in you.

I remember your word.

I thank you for already making a way.

I thank you for peace.

Selah

The wait is over.

You show up God.

You move mountains in my life.

You give far more abundantly and above what I ask for.

You was worth the wait!

Dispense

God will put you in a situation specifically to drop your blessing.

You went to God and prayed on it.

You may feel like God forgot or could not hear you, because Hell breaks out in the areas you prayed for.

It may look like God dropped you,

But in fact..

He is positioning you for the drop of blessings.

So if you feel like God dropped you down a few levels or had some people leave you,

Took away your job, and

Moved you back into your parent's home

do not worry,

This is the time to give God praise!

God had to move some people, places, and things out of the way to make room for what he is giving you.

God dropped you into a place where he can dispense your breakthrough!

Breakthrough

(Declare)

The walls of Jericho are coming DOWN!

Jesus is knocking down barriers and creating a breakthrough in my life!

The limitations are coming DOWN!

The walls people tried to build around me are coming DOWN!

Every wall of a setback the enemy tried to build in front of me is coming DOWN!

Blessings are coming DOWN!

When the walls come down follow Jesus as he leads you out of

Bondage,

negative mindsets,

broken relationships,

Poverty and,

family curses.

This is your time to reap a harvest and to trust God!

Prophesy over yourself that you have the breaker anointing!

Claim your Break through!

Oil Spill

The tipping point.

One more drop of faith is about to cause a supernatural oil spill.

It is going to saturate, overflow, and purify the deepest parts of your soul.

The oil is going to pour over every area of your life.

Supernatural faith is how you accelerate the dropping.

All it takes is one more drop.

Hold on to the promise of God.

Press on.

Let go of distractions and logical thinking.

The oil spill is a sudden move of God.

Do not limit what God can do for you.

Ask God for the impossible.

Prophesy the spilling of oil over your life.

God wants to give you a surplus.

God is waiting on your yes!

Your yes to God is the key to unlocking the spill.

Prepare for the oil spill.

Saturated

We are to be continuously filled with the presence of Jesus.

Pouring into others the sweet love of God, flowing in the spirit.

Rivers of living water.

Waters flowing out of my belly.

A spiritual soaking.

Refreshing anointing.

The overflow.

Jesus soak my spirit with a refreshing outpour,

Not a stream or a creek but an ocean.

Let your Holy Spirit flood, wash, and purify me.

Dear God saturate me in your continuous presence.

Breathe life back into me.

Fill my heart and my mind.

Open my spiritual ears to hear your voice.

Jesus give me wisdom and discernment.

Lead me and let your love pour out of me into others.

Awakened

It was an unusual day.

Something broke through and spoke to my spirit.

Something shifted..

Something deep down rose up.

Suddenly, I could hear GOD calling me..

It was the voice of many waters trickling into my heart.

I could hear my destiny calling.

I knew the voice, but I did not realize it was speaking all along.

Thank you for waking me up.

I am awakening out of this dead slumber.

My spirit leaps.

My soul breathes.

My heart is beating again to the rhythm of the voice of many waters.

My eyes are open.

Jesus is baptizing me in love once again.

The blood of Jesus is running through my veins.

It is purifying me.

I'm in awe as I stand to see the atmosphere of Heaven.

I lift my hands in complete worship to Jesus.

I close my eyes as tears begin to flow.

As I open my eyes I realize,

the Bible is open before me.

I am awakened by each verse I read.

Amber Alert

Sound the alarm.

As you read this, the chains holding you in bondage are breaking and falling off of you.

God is sending out a spiritual amber alert for his children.

You are found in Jesus Christ.

God is sending his angels out to look for you.

Fear not.

You were lost but you are found in God.

The Library of Heaven

God is inviting us into the quiet place.

Through praise and worship we enter in.

We are given access to the library,

a quiet place to study and get to know God.

The library is filled with knowledge and strategies of God's plans.

God is inviting us to come sit with Him.

He wants to reveal the plans He has for His children.

This is where the supernatural download of information takes place.

In the library there is a book with your name on it.

This book has your purpose.

God is waiting to reveal your destiny.

He is waiting for you to come in and spend time with Him.

God wants to share the secrets He has for you.

Just as God has given us the Bible, He also has many books for you.

The books are only found in the library of Heaven.

The Bible was sent to Earth to guide you to the voice of God.

Like the Bible, the books in the library of Heaven lead you to supernatural life.

The Bible is a physical manifestation of the library of Heaven.

When we worship, we enter the secret place with praise on our lips.

Thanking God and giving Him all glory and honor.

God has given us access to the library of Heaven.

Deep within the library is the Throne Room.

To get to the Throne Room requires deeper praise and worship.

Many may get to the library but the chosen ones get to sit at the table in the Throne Room.

The library of Heaven is filled with battle plans, strategies, and specific blue prints.

God is waiting to reveal your purpose to you.

Will you worship God in spirit and truth?

This means you worship God with the fruit of your lips and by reading his Word.

The Bible was not created to collect dust or to open every Sunday.

We are to eat the Word, but you can't eat if you are not hungry!

Ask God for a hunger for his Word.

Will you go in?

God is waiting..

Choose

Glimpse

While I was pregnant I was able to see ultrasounds of my son.

The ultrasound revealed to me what I was about to birth.

My pregnancy became so real to me the moment I was able to see a glimpse of what I was going to birth.

As my pregnancy went on I was able to get more clarity on what was inside of me.

The only way I was able to see what was on the inside of me was through the ultrasound.

Without it I would not have known.

God plants our purpose in us when He designed us, but without Jesus we can't see what is on the inside of us.

It is impossible to know your purpose without knowing Jesus because our purpose is found in Him.

As we grow in our relationship with God, He reveals our purpose and provides a glimpse of what we will birth.

At first it may not look like your purpose and your destiny is coming from certain situations, but trust God.

Keep growing your relationship with Him. He will show you your purpose and lead you to birthing.

Ask God for a glimpse and move by faith until you see it!

Perfect Love

We all have a craving.

When you crave something nothing else will satisfy you

You have to have it.

When you can't get it you become frustrated.

We crave something that for many of us seems hidden.

We try to find it in all the wrong things.

Some people spend their entire lives searching for it and never find it.

So what is it?

What is the craving?

How do we fill the void within our hearts? The void that nothing I tried to fill it with even came close.

The area of us that is covered up with hurt, trauma, pain, loss, rejection, and abandonment.

The missing puzzle piece that you may have looked for in relationships, drugs, sex, weed, a job, a spouse, a child, a career, a family, a gang, drinking, clubbing, traveling, money, a church, or being an entrepreneur.

None of those things fill that longing you feel deep within you.

Emptiness.

Jesus fills the void.

One key unlocks it,

Jesus.

He fills you with perfect love.

It flows like sweet waters hydrating your spirit.

That is why nothing else was able to fill you.

They were temporary.

You were trying to fill your spirit, that is supernatural created by God, with worldly things.

Jesus is the light, hope, and promise that fills you with perfect love.

He gives you access to it.

Perfect love heals and restores you.

Jesus died just to give you perfect love.

Allow Jesus to pour his love into you.

Watering your spirit.

Let God restore you.

Undefeated

Part of finding your identity in Christ is how you live life day to day

Some of us live as if we lost the war

Jesus defeated Satan on the cross already

So why are you living a defeated life?

Ask yourself what do you allow in your life to make you feel defeated

Pray and give it to God

Let it go

You were not created to live:

Depressed

Condemned

Ashamed

Defeated

Guilty

Or unworthy

Those are lies from Satan placed in your life to distract you from your destiny and to keep you from your identity

Your identity is being revealed to you

Satan's identity is being exposed

Jesus is undefeated and that makes us undefeated because Jesus lives on the inside of us

For greater is he that is in me than he that is in the world

Exposing the Enemy

As God reveals you're identity to you he will also expose the enemy.

It is hard to defeat an enemy that is unseen.

Hidden in our daily lives.

We have to be ready because the enemy is studying us.

He is placing traps, tricks, and schemes to deceive us.

We have to ask God to expose the enemy and go to war spiritually.

In the Bible it tells us that we wrestle not against flesh and blood but with spiritual wickedness and powers of darkness in high places.

When you live for God you must be ready for battle.

Put on the whole armor of God every day.

God is sounding the alarm!

God needs us to be in preparation for a spiritual battle

Get into position.

Expose the enemy and conquer the land.

Ask God to expose the enemy in every area of your life.

He is hiding in the things you never thought to look in.

Things you didn't think had to change when you decided to live for God.

He is hinting in the music you allow to enter your mind.

He is hiding in the tv shows you watch through your eyes.

He is hiding in the temptation of forbidden fruit that he tries to get you to taste.

This world is his playground.

He goes around like a hungry lion seeking to devour his prey.

The enemy is looking for an open door to sneak into.

When you expose the door ask God to close it.

Seal it in the blood of Jesus.

Ask the Lord to cover you in the blood of Jesus everyday.

Do not create an opening for the enemy to sneak into.

Your ears are a door.

Your strategy is to be careful of what you listen to.

Your eyes are a door. Be careful of what you watch.

Your mouth is a door. Be careful of what you speak and eat.

Your hands are a door. Be careful of what you do.

Your thoughts are a door. Be careful of what you think.

All of this can seem overwhelming but it is simple.

Pray

Strategically pray and write out specific prayers for every area of your life.

Repent of your sins.

You have to decide to not go back to old things, people, and places.

Chase God.

Ask God to expose the enemy.

Open up your Bible and speak the word of God over you, your family, children, business, finances, etc.

Do this daily to maintain your relationship with God.

Expose the enemy and seal off all open doors.

Pray, fast, and go to God.

Speak the word of God.

If you slip up it is okay.

Repent, that means turn completely away from it and make a decision not to go back to it.

Give it to God and let it go.

Live life victoriously each day and command your victory.

Command your day to be blessed.

Live life using your God given authority over the enemy.

Undefeated!

Identity Thief

Somewhere along the journey you were deceived and lost your identity.

The enemy came in and stole it.

For a lot of us this happened as a child.

The deception comes in many ways.

For some of us the enemy deceived you into believing you were born a certain way and that you can't change.

We are created with our God given identity.

God formed you in your mother's womb.

He created you as a man or a woman.

God makes no mistakes.

You are who God says you are.

The enemy has held your identity for too long.

This is a wakeup call of complete restoration.

Traumatic experiences can could your perception of yourself.

You are not the trauma you went through.

You are not the negative things spoken over you.

Ask God to show you who you are.

Ask God what is your purpose.

Get to know God and you will get to know you because God will reveal it to you.

You may believe you were born a certain way but you can be born again in Jesus Christ.

He died for you.

Take back your identity.

Stop allowing fear, lies, and negative thoughts to confuse you.

You are not a screw up.

You are not an outcast.

You are chosen by God.

You are uniquely and wonderfully made.

You are beautiful/handsome and you have a beautiful mind

Speak life into yourself!

The devil is a liar and a thief who stole your identity but Jesus got it back when he died on the cross!

That false identity the devil tried to force on you is nailed to the cross and crucified with Jesus. It is dead.

You are chosen.

You are anointed.

You were created to live in this lifetime! at this moment!

Smile

You are a gift to the world

Walk in your identity

I prophesy that as you read this God is revealing himself to you and he is revealing your true identity!

Claim it!

Live it!

Walk in it!

Choose.

Deceived

Mind in a fog

Lies on Satan's lips dressed up in your desires

Deception feeding you

The feeling of thinking you are doing everything right

But.. is it from God?

Am I people pleasing?

Confused..

Alone..

Lies from the enemy tempting me to take a bite..

Orphaned pastors leading people to the Father..

Self-ordained pastors, prophets, and ministers leading cults of people in slave mentalities calling it prosperity teachings

Social media scam-prophets lurking for people with itching ears.

Deceiving the saints of their money and pimping the church while they have their Bibles open but speak out of their flesh

Cursing Christians and pastors spewing blessings and curses

People worshiping cash app hungry prophets

People still lost in their own wilderness leading others into the same wildernesses of drug abuse, lust, sleeping with the sheep, etc..

Bibles open and no truth spoken

Christian witches

Living live by horoscopes and God

Living for God and your flesh

Worshiping people and idols of Instagram, Facebook, pornography, money, marriage, and pastors

All deception in different forms

So confusing of what is truth till you open up your Bible for yourself and get to know God.

Finally you see truth.

Do not be deceived.

Ask God for discernment and wisdom.

Read your Bible.

About The Author

Latrice is a talented writer who shares the heart of God with her readers. She enjoys writing poetry that will captivate you while reading each page. Latrice is a resident of Virginia where the blue mountains are painted on the hills. She enjoys spending time with her son, visiting coffee shops, and decorating gift baskets. Latrice is available for book signing and poetry reading.

To reach Latrice Terrell for bookings, poetry readings, or conference email

Latrice.terrell3@gmail.com

www.ingramcontent.com/pod-product-compliance
Lightning Source LLC
Chambersburg PA
CBHW031206160426
43193CB00008B/525